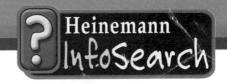

Living by a
River

Heinemann Library
Chicago, Illinois

Carol Baldwin

Customer Service 888-454-2279

Visit our website at www.heinemannlibrary.com

Designed by Kimberly Saar, Heinemann Library
Illustrations and maps by John Fleck
Photo research by Bill Broyles
Printed and bound in the United States by Lake Book Manufacturing, Inc.

07 06 05 04 03
10 9 8 7 6 5 4 3 2 1

Library of Congress Cataloging-in-Publication Data
Baldwin, Carol, 1943-
  Living by a river / Carol Baldwin.
     v. cm. -- (Living habitats)
Includes index.
Contents: What makes water a river? -- Why are rivers important? -- What's green and growing along a river? -- What animals live in and around a river? -- What's for dinner at the river? -- How do river animals get food? -- How do rivers affect people? -- How do people affect rivers? -- Earth's large rivers.
  ISBN 1-40340-842-4 (lib. bdg : hardcover)
  1. Stream ecology--Juvenile literature. [1. Stream ecology. 2. Rivers. 3. Ecology.] I. Title.
  QH541.5.S7 B35 2003
  577.6'4--dc21

                        2002011355

Acknowledgments
The author and publishers are grateful to the following for permission to reproduce copyright material:
p. 4 John Gaps/AP Wide World Photos; p. 5 Michael Fredericks/Animals Animals; p. 6 C.C. Lockwood/Animal Animals; p. 7 Patrick Ward/Corbis; p. 8 Erwin & Peggy Bauer/Animals Animals; p. 9 Francois Gohier/Photo Researchers, Inc.; p. 10 Walt Anderson/Visuals Unlimited; p. 11 Gary Rutherford/Photo Researchers, Inc.; p. 12 Jim Zipp/Photo Researchers, Inc.; p. 13 Milton Tierney/Visuals Unlimited; p. 14 Marie Read/Animals Animals; p. 15 Bertram G. Murray, Jr./Animals Animals; p. 16 Jack Dermid/Photo Researchers, Inc.; p. 17 Douglas Faulkner/Photo Researchers, Inc.; p. 18 Robert Sabin/Animals Animals; p. 20 Tom Bean/Corbis; p. 21 Bruce Brander/Photo Researchers, Inc.; p. 22 Kevin Fleming/Corbis; p. 23 Nigel J.H. Smith/Animals Animals; p. 24 Lester Lefkowitz/Corbis; p. 25 Alexander Lowry/Photo Researchers, Inc.; p. 26 Cameron Davidson; p. 27 John McConnico/AP Wide World Photos

Cover photograph: Geoff Dore/Stone/Getty Images

Every effort has been made to contact copyright holders of any material reproduced in this book. Any omissions will be rectified in subsequent printings if notice is given to the publisher.

Some words are shown in bold, **like this**. You can find out what they mean by looking in the glossary.

Contents

1 What Makes Water a River?

The raging Mississippi River rips a farmhouse from its foundation and carries it away. This is a river. Water slowly flows past a turtle sleeping on a rock. This is a river, too. So, what makes water a river?

It has a beginning

The start of a river is its **source.** Many rivers begin in mountains. Water from **springs,** rainfall, or melting snow runs down the mountain and forms streams. Small streams join to form larger streams. Finally larger streams join to form a river. These larger streams are called **tributaries.**

A river is made of freshwater that flows in a low area called a **channel.** The sides of a river's channel are its **banks.** Every river has a **floodplain** that fills with water when the river **floods.**

Heavy rains can make a river flood.

It has a middle

As a river flows, it tears away soil and small stones from its banks. The water carries this **sediment** through the channel. The wearing away of the land is called **erosion.** A river flowing quickly through steep mountains cuts a V-shaped **valley** into the rocky ground.

This is Stockport Creek, just before it enters the larger Hudson River in New York.

After it leaves the mountains, the river flows through land that is less steep. In this valley, the river slows down and becomes wider. The river channel bends around hills. Tributaries empty more sediment into the river.

The river channel starts to bend from side to side, or **meander.** The water on the inside of bends flows slowly. Here, sediment settles out of the water. Water on the outside of a bend flows more quickly and erodes the banks.

? Did you know?

An oxbow lake is formed when a meandering bend of river is cut off. The river then flows in a straight line instead of around the bend.

It has an end

The river continues to flow slowly toward the ocean. It moves through a wide, flat **floodplain.** It still carries small pieces of sediment called **silt.** After heavy rains, the river **floods.** As water pours onto the floodplain, it drops the silt onto the land. When the flood is over, silt **deposits** remain on the floodplain. The river's banks become higher each year. After a time, the river flows in a **channel** higher than the floodplain.

Lots of channels and small islands make up a river delta.

The place where a river joins an ocean or a lake is called the river **mouth.** Water moves very slowly here and drops more silt. Some rivers, such as the Mississippi and the Nile, drop so much silt that the sea cannot wash it away. It builds up and forms new land, called a **delta.** The river flows over the delta and cuts small channels through it to get to the ocean or lake.

Rivers are important to all living things. People, animals, and plants all use water from rivers in everyday activities.

People use river water for lots of things

People first used rivers to hunt and fish. They used the water for drinking, cooking, and washing. Later, they used the river water to **irrigate** crops they grew along the riverbanks.

Products from many parts of Europe travel along the Rhine River.

Rivers provide transportation

People once used rivers like we use roads. They used boats to travel from one place to another. Cities grew beside rivers because people met there to sell or trade goods. New Orleans is next to the Mississippi River. Today, it receives cotton from farms in Mississippi and lumber from forests in Minnesota.

Rivers are home for plants and animals

Rivers provide homes for many living things. Different kinds of plants and animals live in the water and on the **banks.**

Plants grow in the soft, damp soil of the riverbanks. Some animals, such as bank swallows, dig **burrows** in the banks to live in. Crayfish live on river bottoms. They dig burrows at the bottom of the river. Many kinds of fish, such as trout and catfish, live in rivers. Waterbirds, such as herons and ducks, come to the river to eat. They feed on the animals and plants in the river. River otters eat almost anything they can find. They eat small fish, crayfish, and frogs in the water. They carry bigger fish to the riverbank to eat.

River otters are found in Europe, Asia, Africa, and North and South America.

Giant water lilies grow in the Amazon River. Some of their leaves grow up to six feet (almost two meters) wide.

Different kinds of plants grow in different parts of a river. The types of plants that can grow depend on how fast the water flows.

Attached plants

The bottom is rocky in the upper part of a river. Water flows quickly and carries away anything that is not attached. Green **algae** grows on the rocky bottom. River plants like cushion moss can grow on rocks. The moss gives the rocks a rounder shape and water flows around them.

Rooted and floating plants

In the middle part of the river, water slows down. It drops some of its **sediment.** Here, plants can root and grow. Reeds or cattails grow in the water near the banks.

By the river's **mouth**, the water flows more slowly. Rooted plants grow here, too. Floating plants, like water lilies, can grow without being swept away.

Cottonwood trees grow best in moist soil along rivers and streams.

Trees

In dry places, such as deserts or grasslands, trees may grow only near a river. This is because trees need lots of water to grow. Near rivers, their roots can get enough water from the soil.

In the 1800s, settlers moved west into the treeless grasslands of the United States. They took eastern cottonwood trees with them and planted them along riverbanks. There, the trees could get enough water to grow. Today, you can see winding bands of green trees from an airplane. This tells you where streams and rivers are.

Farm crops

Many farmers grow crops along rivers. The soil there is **fertile.** They can use river water to **irrigate** crops if there isn't enough rain. You might see crops like cotton, sugarcane, rice, potatoes, corn, and wheat along a river.

Different kinds of mangrove trees grow in Florida, Africa, South America, and parts of Asia.

Plants near the river's mouth

Mangrove seeds sprout on the mangrove tree instead of in the ground. This keeps the seeds from being washed away by ocean tides. The seedlings' roots then grow down into the mud. The roots prop the trees up and anchor them in the mud.

Special plants that need the river's floods

Some plants depend on yearly **floods.** Along the Amazon River, water levels can rise as much as 50 feet (about 15 meters). That's as tall as a five-story building. Trees along the Amazon stand in water half the year. Many trees drop their fruits into the water. Fish swimming through the flooded forest eat the fruits. Seeds in the fruits pass through the fishes' digestive systems. When the water level drops, the seeds grow into new trees.

4 What Animals Live in and Around a River?

Some animals, such as fish, live in a river all the time. Others spend only part of their time in the river.

Animals that like fast-moving water

Only a few kinds of animals can live in the rushing water of the upper river. Trout are strong fish. They can swim through the water with their powerful tails. A dipper is a bird that sits on rocks in the river. When it sees an insect, it dives into the water to catch it. It can swim underwater by flapping its wings. Dippers nest among rocks and trees along the river.

Many kinds of insect **larvae** anchor themselves to rocks or plants in the water. This keeps them from being washed down the river.

Dippers spend up to two hours each day walking or swimming under the water.

Gavials are a kind of crocodile. They live along rivers in India. Females lay eggs in nests on the riverbanks.

Animals that like calm water

More animals live where the river moves more slowly. Crayfish hide under stones or weeds in the river during the day. At night, they walk along the river bottom looking for food. Turtles, fish, and frogs also live in calm water.

Reptiles

Some **reptiles,** like alligators and crocodiles, spend lots of time in the river. Nile crocodiles from Africa rest on the **banks** when they're not in the river.

Snapping turtles spend most of their time in rivers. But females leave the water to lay their eggs on dry land. Anacondas, from South America, are one of the world's longest snakes. They can grow up to 30 feet (9 meters) long. They spend most of their lives in slow-moving water.

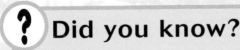 **Did you know?**
There may be as many as five kinds of sharks that live in rivers.

Some animals just find food in the river

Some animals that don't live in the river still need the river in order to live. They depend on it for water, food, and protection.

River otters live in **burrows** in the riverbank. They can move quickly on land and in the water. They often slide headfirst down a muddy bank into the

Belted kingfishers live along rivers and streams in North America.

river. An otter pushes itself along in the water using its tail. It can close its nose and ears when it's in the water searching for food.

Belted kingfishers watch for food from tree branches that hang over the river. When the bird sees a fish or frog, it flies down and dives into the water. It grabs the **prey** with its long bill. A pair of kingfishers will dig a long tunnel in the riverbank. The female lays her eggs at the end of the tunnel.

Hippopotamuses are good swimmers, but they often walk along the bottom of the river. A hippopotamus can hold its breath and stay on the bottom for five minutes.

Big animals

Walking along an African river, you might see a group of hippopotamuses resting in the water. These huge animals can weigh more than a car. Hippos spend up to sixteen hours a day in the water. This helps them keep cool. After the sun sets, hippos leave the river to feed on grass. If they become frightened, they hurry back to the safety of the river.

The water buffalo also cools off in the river. After a swim, it finds a shady spot nearby to rest. At night or early in the morning, it feeds on grass near the river. Then the water buffalo heads back to the river for a drink and a swim.

5 What's for Dinner at the River?

All life, in all **habitats,** begins with plants. Animals eat the plants. Other animals eat the plant-eaters.

Plants

Plants make, or produce, their own food. They are called **producers.** Plants such as water hyacinths, watercress, and pickerel weed are producers that grow in rivers. Water lilies and wild rice are also producers. To make food, plants use carbon dioxide gas in the air and water taken in by their roots. Plants need energy to change the carbon dioxide and water into sugars. The energy comes from sunlight. This process is called **photosynthesis.**

Pickerel weed grows at a river's edge. Ducks and geese eat the seeds of the pickerel weed.

Other producers

Some producers are not plants. **Algae** that grow in fast-moving parts of a river are producers. But they belong to a group of living things called **protists.**

Animals

Animals are called **consumers** because they eat, or consume, food. Some river animals, such as manatees, eat only plants. These animals are called **herbivores.** Other animals, such as snapping turtles and softshell turtles, eat both plants and animals. They are called **omnivores.** Still others, such as crocodiles and anacondas, eat only animals. They are called **carnivores.**

The clean-up crew

Other kinds of consumers feed on dead plants and animals. They are called **decomposers. Bacteria, molds,** and some kinds of beetles are decomposers. Without them, dead plants and animals would pile up everywhere. Decomposers break down **nutrients** stored in dead plants and animals. They put the nutrients back into the soil, air, and water. Plants use the nutrients to help them grow.

Manatees eat only plants that grow in the water.

Some animals hunt other animals. Other animals **scavenge** or **forage.**

Hunting and foraging

Animals that hunt and kill other animals for food are **predators.** Fishing bats are predators. They fly over a river looking for fish. They grab fish from the water with claws on their feet. Animals that predators hunt are called **prey.** Fish are the prey of fishing bats.

Alaskan brown bears gather at rivers to fish for salmon.

Brown bears forage for plants. They feed on leaves, berries, and roots. They also hunt other animals for food. Brown bears are also predators. In summer, salmon swim up rivers to lay their eggs. Brown bears visit the rivers to feed on the salmon. Bears grab the fish with their mouths or their huge claws.

Some river animals are both predators and prey. Salmon eat smaller fish, snails, and crayfish. So, they are predators. However, salmon are also eaten by bears and river otters. So, they are also prey.

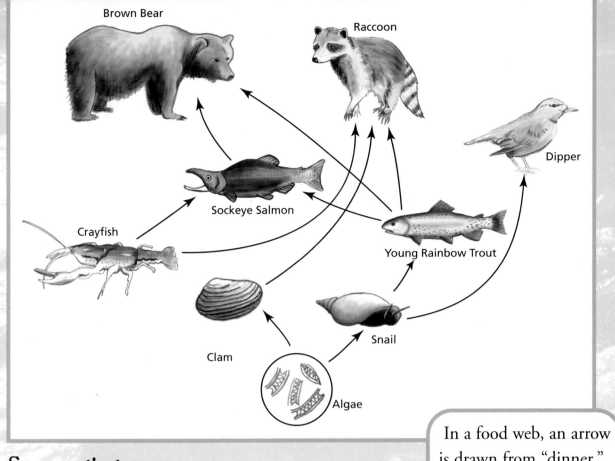

Brown Bear

Raccoon

Dipper

Sockeye Salmon

Crayfish

Young Rainbow Trout

Clam

Snail

Algae

In a food web, an arrow is drawn from "dinner," or prey, and points to the "diner," or predator.

Scavenging

Crayfish and catfish scavenge for food. They eat decaying plant and animal material in the river.

Planning the menu

The path that shows who eats what is a **food chain.** All living things are parts of food chains. In the river, snails eat algae. Then, young trout eat snails. Salmon eat young trout. Finally, bears eat salmon. .

Another river food chain includes algae, clams, and birds called dippers. Algae are in another river food chain that includes snails, young trout, and raccoons. Several food chains that are connected make up a **food web.**

7 How Do Rivers Affect People?

Heavy rains or melting snow can cause a river to flow over its **banks.** This causes a **flood.** Along rivers like the Mississippi, most floods happen in the spring.

Rivers can flood homes and farms

In 1993, people in Grafton, Illinois, had watched the rising Mississippi River for days. They knew a big flood was coming. Some had packed their things and moved to higher ground. Soon, brown river water rushed through the streets. It flowed into homes and stores.

Outside the town, farmers watched their fields turn into lakes. Their young corn and soybean plants drowned.

Living in a **floodplain** can be both good and bad. The **fertile** soil of the Mississippi floodplain is good for growing crops. But a flood could destroy both the crops and the farm buildings.

Rivers can harm or help crops

The Ganges is the most important river in India. Most of its **floodplain** has been cleared of **native** grasses and trees. Crops, such as rice and potatoes, are grown there instead. During the summer rainy season, heavy rains sometimes cause floods that destroy the crops.

Floods near Dhaka, Bangladesh, destroy crops and homes.

Other rivers, like the Amazon and the Nile, flood at the same time every year. People who live along these rivers plan for these floods. They plant crops after the water level drops.

What is a flash flood?

Some floods happen quickly as a result of heavy rainstorms. These sudden floods are called **flash floods.** They usually last only a few hours. But they can be very dangerous. Their raging waters move very fast. Sometimes people have little time to escape. Few places are completely safe from flash floods. In a desert, a rainstorm can quickly fill a dry canyon.

Rivers help cities develop

If you look at a world map, you will see that many cities are next to rivers. The world's first **cultures** developed along the banks of rivers. The Nile is Egypt's only river. In ancient Egypt, the Nile River's yearly **floods** made the soil good for farming. People also fished in the river. They used the river to carry materials for building monuments. The huge blocks of stone that were used to build the pyramids traveled on boats down the Nile.

People depend on the Nile's water for many things.

Today, Cairo is Egypt's largest city. It is near the **mouth** of the Nile. The Nile still affects life in Egypt. Boats still carry goods along the river. Farmers grow crops such as cotton, wheat, dates, and sugarcane. They **irrigate** the crops with the river's water. And people still catch fish from the river for food.

The Ganges River has been used for trade and travel since early times. The city of Calcutta, India, grew near the river's mouth. Many ships that trade with India come to Calcutta to load and unload their goods.

People live above flood water

Along the Amazon River, most people live in areas that flood every year. Their small homes are built on tall poles to avoid the water. Only the soil near the river is **fertile** enough to grow crops every year. People grow corn and **manioc.** Crops are planted and grown when the water level is low. People hunt in the forest and fish in the river. They raise pigs and chickens. When the water level rises, people use boats to get around. They move their animals into their houses or keep them safe on floating platforms.

During the dry season along the Amazon River, people use ladders to climb up to their homes.

23

How Do People Affect Rivers?

People need to protect rivers, but this doesn't always happen. Many times people harm rivers.

Dams are built

People build dams on rivers for several reasons. Dams are built across rivers to stop the water from flowing. They help control river flooding. The water forms a lake behind the dam. People and animals that lived there have to move away as the lake fills. Water from the new lake can be used to **irrigate** crops and for drinking water for people living in cities.

Electricity is made

Dams also are used to make electricity. Many dams have gates that can be opened to let water flow out of the lake. As the water rushes through the gates, it turns the blades of a **turbine.** The spinning turbine helps make electricity.

Today, there are about 40,000 large dams around the world.

Dams change rivers

Dams can also cause problems. **Sediment,** which is needed to make soil **fertile,** collects behind a dam. The river cannot transport it to the soil along its channel. Changing a river's flow can also destroy wildlife **habitats.** Dry-land plants may die as the new lake is formed. Animals that lived there have to move away or they will die, too.

Aqueducts carry water from rivers to cities hundreds of miles away.

The water is taken away

In the western United States, many cities use water from the Colorado River. Large amounts of river water are sent to big cities such as Los Angeles in California and Phoenix in Arizona. Farmers also use some river water to **irrigate** crops. The Colorado River used to flow into the Gulf of California. Now, too much water is taken from the river. Most of the time, the river dries up before it reaches the Gulf.

People destroy floodplains

Many plants and animals are **adapted** to live in **floodplains.** Along the Mississippi, black willow trees can have their trunks and lower branches underwater for weeks without damage. Flood waters leave behind small pools of water on the floodplain. These pools hold water through the spring and summer. Frogs and toads need these pools to lay their eggs.

Building towns and cities on river floodplains destroys **habitats** for plants and animals. The pavement of city streets and parking lots keeps rain water from soaking into the ground. This means that more water flows into the rivers. During heavy rains, this can cause more flooding. People build **levees** to protect river towns. Levees hold back rivers and keep them from flooding the towns. However, if levees break, the flooding can be much worse.

Many towns were flooded in 1993, when the Mississippi River broke through levees.

The water of the Ganges River has been damaged by sewage pollution.

People and factories pollute river water

Today, many rivers around the world are damaged by **pollution.** Waste water from homes is called **sewage.** In some countries, sewage is dumped into rivers. Factories may use lots of river water. They may pump the water back into rivers. Sometimes, this water is hot, or has **chemicals** in it. Chemicals from farm fields also get washed into rivers.

Water that is too warm kills many kinds of living things. Chemicals can also kill river plants and animals. False map turtles live in North American rivers. Harmful chemicals dumped into rivers have killed the snails and clams that the turtles eat. Giant river otters and pink dolphins live in the Amazon River. They are being killed by pollution from gold mines. These are only some of many river animals that are harmed by pollution.

Fact File

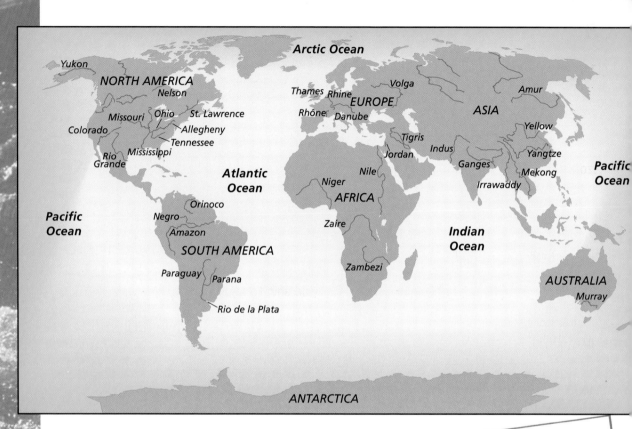

Some of the major rivers of the world are shown on this map. But there are hundreds of small rivers all over the world that are also important. Just like big rivers, they are home to many plants and animals. Small rivers are also used and enjoyed by people who live near them or visit them.

In the United States, the National Rivers Inventory lists more than 3,400 segments, or parts, of rivers that are important because of the natural area they are in or because of the local culture. These segments can be as short as four miles (about six kilometers) long or they can be hundreds of miles long.

Earth's Large Rivers

River	Continent	Facts
Nile	Africa	Longest river in the world; has a large delta where it empties into the Mediterranean Sea.
Amazon	South America	Carries one-fifth of the world's fresh water to the sea—up to 32 million gallons (121 million liters) a second; no bridges cross the river.
Mississippi-Missouri	North America	At its source in Lake Itasca, Minnesota, the Mississippi River is only 12 feet (4 meters) wide and 18 inches (46 centimeters) deep.
Yangtze-Kiang	Asia	The building of a large dam will force up to 2 million people from their homes.
Ganges	Asia	Many of the 300 million people living along the river believe it is holy.
Murray-Darling	Australia	A huge irrigation project allows crops to be grown along the lower 400 miles (644 kilometers) of the river.
Congo (Zaire)	Africa	Large boats can't travel on about 250 miles (400 kilometers) of the river because there are more than 4,000 islands in the river.
Hwang He	Asia	The worst flood in modern times occurred on this river in 1931. About 80 million people lost their homes and about 1 million people died.
Rhine	Europe	It is the busiest river in Europe. Rotterdam, at the mouth of the river, is the world's busiest port.
Mackenzie	North America	The river flows into the Arctic Ocean. It is frozen from November to June.

Glossary

adapted changed to live under certain conditions

algae group of tiny living things that live in water and make their own food

aqueduct large pipe or channel built to carry water over a long distance

bacteria living things too small to be seen except with a microscope

bank high ground that borders a river, also called a riverbank

burrow hole dug in the ground by animals for shelter

carnivore animal that eats only other animals

channel low area through which a river flows

chemical any substance which can change when mixed with another substance

consumer living thing that needs plants for food

culture customs, arts, and buildings of a group of people

decomposer consumer that puts nutrients from dead plants and animals back into the soil, air, and water

delta land that is formed where a river empties sediments into a lake or ocean

deposits materials left behind. River deposits include silt, sand, and stones.

erosion movement of soil and rocks by water, wind, or ice

fertile able to produce crops easily

flash flood sudden flood caused by very heavy rains

flood great flow of water over what is usually dry land

floodplain flat area on either side of a river. A flooding river covers this area.

food chain path that shows who eats what in a habitat

food web group of connected food chains in a habitat

forage wander about in search of food

habitat place where a plant or animal lives

herbivore animal that eats only plants

irrigate supply the land with water

larvae young of insects

levee high wall made of dirt that is built along the banks of a river to stop it from flooding

manioc tropical plant that is used to make a kind of flour

meander follow a winding course

mold living thing that uses dead plants and animals for food. Molds are decomposers.

mouth part of a river where water empties into a lake or ocean

native born, grown, or produced in a certain place

nutrient material that is needed for growth of a plant or animal

omnivore animal that eats plants and animals

photosynthesis process by which green plants trap the sun's energy and use it to change carbon dioxide and water into sugars

pollution harmful materials in the water, air, or land

predator animal that hunts and eats other animals

prey animal that is hunted and eaten by other animals

producer living thing that can use sunlight to make its own food

protist type of living thing that is neither a plant nor an animal. Algae are protists.

reptile type of animal that includes turtles, snakes, lizards, crocodiles, and alligators

scavenge feed on the bodies of dead animals

sediment tiny bits of rocks, sand, and soil

sewage waste water from homes

silt very fine bits of mud and sand carried along and then dropped by river water

source place where a river begins

spring place where underground water comes to the surface

tributaries streams or rivers that flow into a larger river

turbine wheel with many curved blades

valley low land lying between hills

More Books to Read

Dramer, Kim. *The Mekong River.* Danbury, Conn.: Franklin Watts, 2001.

Fink Martin, Patricia A. *Exploring Ecosystems: Rivers and Streams.* Danbury, Conn.: Franklin Watts, 1999.

Fleisher, Paul. *Webs of Life: Mountain Stream.* Salt Lake City, Utah: Benchmark Books, 1999.

Parker, Steve. *Eyewitness: Pond and River.* New York: DK Publishing, 2000.

Rawlins, Carol B. *The Colorado River.* Danbury, Conn.: Franklin Watts, 1999.

Rawlins, Carol B. *The Seine River.* Danbury, Conn.: Franklin Watts, 2001.

Whitcraft, Melissa. *The Niagara River.* Danbury, Conn.: Franklin Watts, 2001.

Index